The Second Coming Of Entrepreneurial Branding For A New Era Marketplace

The Basics Of New Era Rebranding
For Repositioning & Relaunching
Your Brand Or Business With Online Media Tours
(Action Planner)

AliNICOLE "WATERS"

The Second Coming Of Entrepreneurial Branding For A New Era Marketplace

Ask Yourself...

What do I most need to honor about my brand or business in the present?

Are there any aspects from the old and/or current frameworks of my branding that can support my next level?

What aspects of my current mission do I need to turn the volume down on in order to learn my NEW ERA VOICE & BRAND MISSION?

What is my NEW ERA MARKETPLACE BRANDING FACTOR?

What is mine to learn about the new era marketplace and how do I best

prepare?

What areas should I start on as it relates to the rebranding process for the new era marketplace?

I'm wondering how to currently start bridging the gap and operate from both sides of the tracks as I'm shifting more into the new?

The Basics Of Creating An Online Rebranding Media Tour

* Create A Theme: This can be the name of your tour.

* Define Your Tour: What type of branding or rebranding online media tour are you planning to launch?

* Create A Core Objective: The purpose or intention of your tour and what it's designed to accomplish for your brand, business, and audience.

* Create Three Primary Areas Of Focuses: These can be in the form of goals that are high-level priorities for achieving during each phase.

* Decide The Dates & Time Frames Of Your Tour: Write everything down on a separate calendar.

* Enroll Assistance (Optional): Decide early on in the process if you will need help and set up a support system to help you with endeavors at every phase.

* Decide The Formats/Methods & Explore Platforms To Host Your Tour: Will it be a combination of blog tours, guest blogging, media blitz, podcast features, Facebook pages, print-press features, webinar series or more? (Consider hosting your tour on a platform like Tumblr).

* Create A Three-Tier Offer Options: Create a small, medium, and high-end offer to cover different price-points.

* Create A Plan Of Action: Set aside a planner that will only contain your online branding media tour agenda.

* Launch Your Tour: Market, Market, Market Your New Branding Point Of View!

* Create A Post Tour Plan (Optional): Rinse, Repeat Or Repurpose Your Tour As An Evergreen Offer.

The Second Coming Of Your Entrepreneurial Branding

Rebranding for the new era marketplace begins with examining your branding evolutionary journey, understanding the new era marketplace, and its consumers in addition to becoming aware of your emerging tribe and unique NEW ERA VOICE. It's from this discovery that you're able to accurately prepare and position yourself effectively for the emerging new era changes.

Bridging the gap between the old and the new isn't always easy and especially when the business world is being faced with an emerging phenomenon that has never occurred in the history of business and branding. This new phenomenon is called the NEW ERA MARKETPLACE TRAJECTORY. The new era marketplace is metaphorically considered to be the NEW EARTH of the business world. Several businesses, corporations, organizations, and more will begin to see a massive shift take place as they witness their operations either being rapture-ed into the full expansion of their next-levels of greatness or to experience what will seem like business marketplace ARMAGEDDON.

Either way, rebranding for the new era is going to be required and also education for this next dimension of the new info structure, reconstruction, and renovation of a new business world and more. If a brand is left behind and doesn't rebrand or level up enough for the new era, it's going to be almost impossible to resurrect or relaunch that brand or business again even if it's rebuilt with what would seem to be the best solid plan.

If that plan doesn't fall under the new era marketplace expansion, the success of that operation will be short-lived. Rebranding won't be optional, neither will not becoming aligned with the new era marketplace requirements. This starts with turning down the volume on one's current mission so that they can hear their NEW ERA VOICE & MISSION. The current mission is no longer the BIG THING and must be repositioned for greater expansion. This doesn't mean that all of the old or current mission is going away, it just means that it can no longer be the chief cornerstone of one's brand, business, or mission.

So often, brands and businesses stay stuck on their current mission that was birthed from an old part of their journey. Because of this, it doesn't allow them to step into a new dimension of their evolutionary expansion as a brand and/or empire expression. The more one continues to regurgitate the WHAT-WASNESS of their journey believing that it should continue to be the umbrella-focal point of their new innovation, the more they do a huge disservice to their brand and audience.

Failing to evolve one's story and mission will only keep brands and businesses stuck in what I call brand buffering which is a holding pattern of loading but never fully making the connection. I'm not implying that one should completely abandon their current mission or signature offerings, however, as mentioned previously, again, the volume needs to be turned down on it in order to hear the NEW ERA VOICE coming forth.

This is where the next-level uniqueness resides and rebranding begins to take place. I call this the Second Coming of one's entrepreneurial branding. A new demonstration of the evolution of one's brand is required in order to catapult their success and unique branding factor. Again, this type of rebranding doesn't always consist of fully letting go of the current WHAT-IS-NESS, however, as mention previously, it just gets repositioned into its proper place. Trust me your current voice is not your NEW ERA VOICE or UNIQUENESS. Often times, your current audience i not your new era audience, however, they can be leveled up to embrace the newness that will come forth from you and join you with your new emerging tribe.

Your NEW ERA VOICE and UNIQUENESS will start to reveal to you who your emerging tribe is and how to best prepare for them. Once you honor this process you will begin to see even more breakthroughs and results like never before from your current and older works. As this process unfolds a new overarching umbrella for your rebranding factor will start to emerge to create the new. It's from this new vantage point will you be able to accurately prepare and serve your current and emerging audience at the highest levels.

The process of leveling up one's brand or rebranding can be an exciting yet challenging experience if not accurately planned for effective execution. I have found over the years that online media tours are extremely helpful for brand or rebranding launches. Online media tours also work great for products and book launches or even virtual speaking series.

The Second Coming Of Entrepreneurial Branding For A New Era Marketplace

These endeavors work best when conducted over a series of weeks or months and broken down into phases with a core theme and primary focuses for each stage of the tour. If you are a high-end brand or high-end service provider that doesn't normally serve outside the high-ticket sales, this format will work well for creating new offers or creating an evergreen platform that can service several price-points to make a greater impact.

I've found that even going through the process leading up to the actual launch, can open you up into a new realm of infinite possibilities that weren't even on the radar that can be lucrative and leveraging with what you're already doing. It's really unexplainable and just has to be experienced. This becomes the ultimate branding game-changer and most do better with one media tour than they do in an entire year in their business.

The benefits of an online media rebranding tour...

* It helps to transition your brand with ease and is done in phases to reintroduce you as a brand to your current audience or to the next level of your offerings. This also works best for introducing a new audience to your branding.

* It helps to leverage your time for creating a residual income at various price-points with new offers while experiencing other lucrative opportunities.

* It allows you to revamp your online/social media presence and/or methods.

* It works great in concert with an actual LIVE media branding tour or works great as a lead-in to your live endeavors.

*It provides several audiences with options that will allow you to serve them at various levels and price points.

This action planner is designed to assist you with discovering your New Era VOICE, unique new branding factor, relevant mission, and online media tour creation. Use the action planner page to create the second coming of your brand with online media tours.

The Second Coming Of Entrepreneurial Branding For A New Era Marketplace

Start discovering your NEW ERA VOICE & UNIQUENESS
by asking yourself...

What aspects of my current mission do I need to turn down the volume on and start repositioning?

What is wanting to emerge from my branding at this phase?

How can I best prepare for the emerging new era marketplace shift?

What is my NEW ERA VOICE?

I'm curious to know what my NEW ERA UNIQUE Factor is?

What does the Second Coming of my branding look like at this phase?

What are my next best steps for rebranding with my new profound knowledge?

Asking and answering these questions with a rinse and repeat routine will help you to start leveling-up in a new way and provide insights for how to move forward in the most effective way for rebranding, repositioning, and relaunching.

The Second Coming Of Entrepreneurial Branding For A New Era Marketplace

The Second Coming Of My Entrepreneurial Branding Online Media Tour
Action Planning Section

ON TOUR SOON!!!!!!!!!

Use the action planning space below to design your online media tours.

The Second Coming Of Entrepreneurial Branding For A New Era Marketplace

The Second Coming Of Entrepreneurial Branding For A New Era Marketplace

NOW ON TOUR!!!!!!!!!!!!!!!!!!

Record your online media process and results.

ON TOUR SOON!!!!!!!!!

Use the action planning space below to design your online media tours.

The Second Coming Of Entrepreneurial Branding For A New Era Marketplace

The Second Coming Of Entrepreneurial Branding For A New Era Marketplace

NOW ON TOUR!!!!!!!!!!!!!!!!!!!

Record your online media process and results.

The Second Coming Of Entrepreneurial Branding For A New Era Marketplace

ON TOUR SOON!!!!!!!!!

Use the action planning space below to design your online media tours.

The Second Coming Of Entrepreneurial Branding For A New Era Marketplace

The Second Coming Of Entrepreneurial Branding For A New Era Marketplace

NOW ON TOUR!!!!!!!!!!!!!!!!!!

Record your online media process and results.

The Second Coming Of Entrepreneurial Branding For A New Era Marketplace

ON TOUR SOON!!!!!!!!!

Use the action planning space below to design your online media tours.

The Second Coming Of Entrepreneurial Branding For A New Era Marketplace

The Second Coming Of Entrepreneurial Branding For A New Era Marketplace

NOW ON TOUR!!!!!!!!!!!!!!!!!!!

Record your online media process and results.

The Second Coming Of Entrepreneurial Branding For A New Era Marketplace

ON TOUR SOON!!!!!!!!!

Use the action planning space below to design your online media tours.

The Second Coming Of Entrepreneurial Branding For A New Era Marketplace

Continued Planning

The Second Coming Of Entrepreneurial Branding For A New Era Marketplace

NOW ON TOUR!!!!!!!!!!!!!!!!!

Record your online media process and results.

The Second Coming Of Entrepreneurial Branding For A New Era Marketplace

ON TOUR SOON!!!!!!!!!

Use the action planning space below to design your online media tours.

The Second Coming Of Entrepreneurial Branding For A New Era Marketplace

NOW ON TOUR!!!!!!!!!!!!!!!!!!

Record your online media process and results.

The Second Coming Of Entrepreneurial Branding For A New Era Marketplace

ON TOUR SOON!!!!!!!!!

Use the action planning space below to design your online media tours.

The Second Coming Of Entrepreneurial Branding For A New Era Marketplace

The Second Coming Of Entrepreneurial Branding For A New Era Marketplace

NOW ON TOUR!!!!!!!!!!!!!!!!!!

Record your online media process and results.

The Second Coming Of Entrepreneurial Branding For A New Era Marketplace

ON TOUR SOON!!!!!!!!!

Use the action planning space below to design your online media tours.

The Second Coming Of Entrepreneurial Branding For A New Era Marketplace

NOW ON TOUR!!!!!!!!!!!!!!!!!!!

Record your online media process and results.

The Second Coming Of Entrepreneurial Branding For A New Era Marketplace

ON TOUR SOON!!!!!!!!!

Use the action planning space below to design your online media tours.

The Second Coming Of Entrepreneurial Branding For A New Era Marketplace

The Second Coming Of Entrepreneurial Branding For A New Era Marketplace

NOW ON TOUR!!!!!!!!!!!!!!!!!!

Record your online media process and results.

The Second Coming Of Entrepreneurial Branding For A New Era Marketplace

ON TOUR SOON!!!!!!!!!

Use the action planning space below to design your online media tours.

The Second Coming Of Entrepreneurial Branding For A New Era Marketplace

NOW ON TOUR!!!!!!!!!!!!!!!!!!

Record your online media process and results.

ON TOUR SOON!!!!!!!!!

Use the action planning space below to design your online media tours.

The Second Coming Of Entrepreneurial Branding For A New Era Marketplace

Continued Planning

The Second Coming Of Entrepreneurial Branding For A New Era Marketplace

NOW ON TOUR!!!!!!!!!!!!!!!!!!

Record your online media process and results.

The Second Coming Of Entrepreneurial Branding For A New Era Marketplace

ON TOUR SOON!!!!!!!!!

Use the action planning space below to design your online media tours.

The Second Coming Of Entrepreneurial Branding For A New Era Marketplace

The Second Coming Of Entrepreneurial Branding For A New Era Marketplace

NOW ON TOUR!!!!!!!!!!!!!!!!!!

Record your online media process and results.

The Second Coming Of Entrepreneurial Branding For A New Era Marketplace

ON TOUR SOON!!!!!!!!!

Use the action planning space below to design your online media tours.

The Second Coming Of Entrepreneurial Branding For A New Era Marketplace

The Second Coming Of Entrepreneurial Branding For A New Era Marketplace

NOW ON TOUR!!!!!!!!!!!!!!!!!!

Record your online media process and results.

The Second Coming Of Entrepreneurial Branding For A New Era Marketplace

ON TOUR SOON!!!!!!!!!

Use the action planning space below to design your online media tours.

The Second Coming Of Entrepreneurial Branding For A New Era Marketplace

NOW ON TOUR!!!!!!!!!!!!!!!!!!

Record your online media process and results.

The Second Coming Of Entrepreneurial Branding For A New Era Marketplace

ON TOUR SOON!!!!!!!!!

Use the action planning space below to design your online media tours.

The Second Coming Of Entrepreneurial Branding For A New Era Marketplace

The Second Coming Of Entrepreneurial Branding For A New Era Marketplace

NOW ON TOUR!!!!!!!!!!!!!!!!!

Record your online media process and results.

The Second Coming Of Entrepreneurial Branding For A New Era Marketplace

ON TOUR SOON!!!!!!!!!

Use the action planning space below to design your online media tours.

The Second Coming Of Entrepreneurial Branding For A New Era Marketplace

The Second Coming Of Entrepreneurial Branding For A New Era Marketplace

NOW ON TOUR!!!!!!!!!!!!!!!!!!

Record your online media process and results.

The Second Coming Of Entrepreneurial Branding For A New Era Marketplace

More Notes

More Notes

For More Related Resources
Visit:
www.thesecondcomingofbranding.tumblr.com

Visit Author's Page for More
Resources for Different Industries
www.amazon.com/author/alicianwaters

To Book Author for Speaking Engagements

Email: anwempires@gmail.com

If you enjoyed this resource, please consider writing a review on
Amazon.com.

Thanks & Blessings!